How to Analyze the Works of

WILLIAM
SHAKESPEARE

by Mari Kesselring

ABDO
Publishing Company

Essential Critiques

How to Analyze the Works of

WILLIAM SHAKESPEARE

by Mari Kesselring

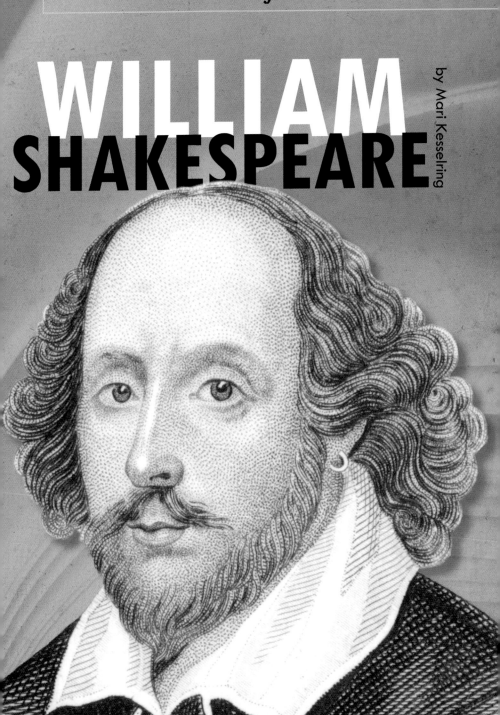

Content Consultant: Marcela Kostihova,
Associate Professor, Department of English, Hamline University

Credits

Published by ABDO Publishing Company, PO Box 398166, Minneapolis, MN 55439. Copyright © 2013 by Abdo Consulting Group, Inc. International copyrights reserved in all countries. No part of this book may be reproduced in any form without written permission from the publisher. The Essential Library™ is a trademark and logo of ABDO Publishing Company.

Printed in the United States of America,
North Mankato, Minnesota
042012
092012

 THIS BOOK CONTAINS AT LEAST 10% RECYCLED MATERIALS.

Editor: Lauren Coss
Series Designer: Marie Tupy

Library of Congress Cataloging-in-Publication Data
Kesselring, Mari.
  How to analyze the works of William Shakespeare / Mari Kesselring.
    p. cm. -- (Essential critiques)
  Includes bibliographical references.
  ISBN 978-1-61783-460-8
  1. Shakespeare, William, 1564-1616--Criticism and interpretation. I. Title.
  PR2976.K48 2012
  822.3'3--dc23
                                                    2012005974

Table of Contents

Chapter

1

Introduction to Critiques

What Is Critical Theory?

What do you usually do when you read a book? You probably absorb the specific language style of the book. You learn about the characters as they are developed through thoughts, dialogue, and other interactions. You may like or dislike a character more than others. You might be drawn in by the plot of the book, eager to find out what happens at the end. Yet these are only a few of many possible ways of understanding and appreciating a book. What if you are interested in delving more deeply? You might want to learn more about the author and how his or her personal background is reflected in the book. Or you might want to examine what the book says about society—how it depicts the roles of

women and minorities, for example. If so, you have entered the realm of critical theory.

Critical theory helps you learn how various works of art, literature, music, theater, film, and other endeavors either support or challenge the way society behaves. Critical theory is the evaluation and interpretation of a work using different philosophies, or schools of thought. Critical theory can be used to understand all types of cultural productions.

There are many different critical theories. If you are analyzing literature, each theory asks you to look at the work from a different perspective. Some theories address social issues, while others focus on the writer's life or the time period in which the book was written or set. For example, the critical theory that asks how an author's life affected the work is called biographical criticism. Other common schools of criticism include historical criticism, feminist criticism, psychological criticism, and New Criticism, which examines a work solely within the context of the work itself.

What Is the Purpose of Critical Theory?

Critical theory can open your mind to new ways of thinking. It can help you evaluate a book from a new perspective, directing your attention to issues and messages you may not otherwise recognize in a work. For example, applying feminist criticism to a book may make you aware of female stereotypes perpetuated in the work. Applying a critical theory to a book helps you learn about the person who created it or the society that enjoyed it. You can also explore how the work is perceived by current cultures.

How Do You Apply Critical Theory?

You conduct a critique when you use a critical theory to examine and question a work. The theory you choose is a lens through which you can view the work, or a springboard for asking questions about the work. Applying a critical theory helps you think critically about the work. You are free to question the work and make an assertion about it. If you choose to examine a book using biographical theory, for example, you want to know how the author's personal background or education inspired or shaped the work. You could explore why the author was drawn to the story. For instance, are there any parallels between a particular character's life and the author's life?

Forming a Thesis

Ask your question and find answers in the work or other related materials. Then you can create a thesis. The thesis is the key point in your critique. It is your argument about the work based on the tenets, or beliefs, of the theory you are using. For example, if you are using biographical theory to ask how the author's life inspired the work, your thesis could be worded as follows: Writer Teng Xiong, raised in refugee camps in

> ### How to Make a Thesis Statement
>
> In a critique, a thesis statement typically appears at the end of the introductory paragraph. It is usually only one sentence long and states the author's main idea.

southeast Asia, drew upon her experiences to write the novel *No Home for Me*.

Providing Evidence

Once you have formed a thesis, you must provide evidence to support it. Evidence might take the form of examples and quotes from the work itself—such as dialogue from a character. Articles about the book or personal interviews with the author might also support your ideas. You may wish to address what other critics have written about the work. Quotes from these individuals may help support your claim. If you find any quotes or examples that contradict your thesis, you will need to create an argument against them. For instance: Many critics have pointed to the protagonist of *No Home for Me* as a powerless victim of circumstances. However, in the chapter "My Destiny," she is clearly depicted as someone who seeks to shape her own future.

How to Support a Thesis Statement

A critique should include several arguments. Arguments support a thesis claim. An argument is one or two sentences long and is supported by evidence from the work being discussed.

Organize the arguments into paragraphs. These paragraphs make up the body of the critique.

In This Book

In this book, you will read
summaries of famous plays by
writer William Shakespeare,
each followed by a critique. Each
critique will use one theory and
apply it to one work. Critical
thinking sections will give you a
chance to consider other theses and
questions about the work. Did you
agree with the author's application
of the theory? What other questions
are raised by the thesis and its
arguments? You can also find out
what other critics think about each
particular book. Then, in the You Critique It section
in the final pages of this book, you will have an
opportunity to create your own critique.

Look for the Guides

Throughout the chapters
that analyze the works,
thesis statements have been
highlighted. The box next to
the thesis helps explain what
questions are being raised
about the work. Supporting
arguments have been
underlined. The boxes next to
the arguments help explain
how these points support the
thesis. Look for these guides
throughout each critique.

Essential Critiques

William Shakespeare's works have influenced society for more than 400 years.

2

A Closer Look at William Shakespeare

Although William Shakespeare lived more than 400 years ago, most people today are familiar with his work. A total of 37 plays are attributed to Shakespeare, as well as many sonnets and longer poems. Shakespeare's life and works have inspired many modern films and books.

Because Shakespeare lived so long ago, we know very little about his life. Some scholars maintain Shakespeare was not the man we have always believed he was. Different theories claim the real author of the works attributed to Shakespeare was the Earl of Oxford, the Earl of Southampton, poet Francis Bacon, or even Queen Elizabeth.

There are only a handful of surviving mentions of Shakespeare and his family. Much of what we know about the writer is based on assumptions and educated guesses about the time and place in which he lived.

Childhood

William Shakespeare was born approximately 100 miles (161 km) from London, England, in the town Stratford-upon-Avon. He was baptized on April 26, 1564. Most people believe he was born on April 23, since it is likely he was baptized just a few days after his birth. William was born during a period known as the Renaissance, a European cultural movement that focused on the rebirth of art, literature, and science. The Renaissance began in Italy, and by the sixteenth century it had spread to England.

Young William had seven siblings, three of whom died during childhood. William may have attended a local grammar school to learn to read and write.

Shakespeare's Family

In 1582, when Shakespeare was 18 years old, he married Anne Hathaway. Anne was eight years older than him and already several months pregnant with their first child. Their marriage was probably put together quickly. If Anne had been unmarried when the baby was born, she would have faced harsh criticism and possible punishment from her community. It was unusual at that time for a middle-class man, such as Shakespeare, to marry so young. It was also rare for a man to marry a woman who was so much older than him. The couple's first child, Susanna, was born in May 1583. Two years later, Anne gave birth to twins — a boy named Hamnet and a girl named Judith. Hamnet died in 1596, when he was 11 years old.

The Playwright

After the birth of Shakespeare's twins, there is an almost ten-year gap with no written record of what was happening in his life. The next surviving mention of Shakespeare is from 1592, when rival playwright Robert Greene wrote bitterly of the popularity and success of a newcomer, Shakespeare, on London's stages. It is not known exactly when or why Shakespeare traveled to London and started writing plays. But, most scholars deduce that in the mid-1580s, when Shakespeare was in his early twenties, he left Stratford-upon-Avon and traveled to London. By 1594, Shakespeare was listed as a member in the theater group Lord Chamberlain's

Men. Shakespeare would be with the theater group for the rest of his time in London. In 1599, the group raised enough money to build their own theater in Southwark, England, a suburb of London. The new theater was called the Globe, and Shakespeare was one of the main investors in the enterprise.

The Complete Works

The exact order in which Shakespeare wrote his plays is not known. However, scholars have made guesses. They believe Shakespeare first wrote plays about British history, such as *Richard III*, and comedic plays, such as *The Taming of the Shrew*, in the early 1590s. He may have also written his most well-known narrative poems, *Venus and Adonis* and *The Rape of Lucrece*, during the early 1590s. Scholars believe by the late 1590s Shakespeare was working on many of his most popular comedies, including *As You Like It*. He is also believed to have written some of his best-known histories during this time, including *Henry V*. In the early 1600s, Shakespeare began shifting his focus toward writing tragedies, including *Hamlet* and *Othello*. A collection of Shakespeare's sonnets was printed in 1609, though it is unclear when he wrote them.

Shakespeare's plays are still performed at the Globe Theater in London.

By 1610, Shakespeare was once again writing more light-hearted plays, such as *The Tempest*.

Death and Legacy

As early as 1612, Shakespeare moved from London and retired in Stratford-upon-Avon. In March 1616, he made some changes to his will. He died on April 23, 1616. He was buried at the Holy Trinity church in Stratford-upon-Avon, a site that can still be visited today.

Shakespeare's works are still performed around the world. He is often credited with adding many popular words and phrases to the English vocabulary. Shakespeare has made a large impact on society and art that cannot be forgotten.

Actress Claire Danes played Juliet in a 1996 film adaptation of *Romeo and Juliet*.

Chapter

3

An Overview of
Romeo and Juliet

Romeo and Juliet takes place in Verona, Italy. Two noble families of Verona, the Montagues and the Capulets, have an ancient grudge that has often led to unrest in the city.

Act 1

As the play begins, two servants for the Capulets enter the stage. One is bragging about how he will fight any Montague. Two Montague servants enter. The insults quickly escalate, and all the men draw their swords.

Benvolio, Montague's nephew, enters and tries to break up the brawl. Tybalt, a nephew of Capulet, also arrives and joins the fight. Capulet, head of the Capulet family, and Lady Capulet arrive, responding to the disturbance, followed by Montague, head of the Montague family, and Lady Montague. Finally, the Prince of Verona, Escalus, appears. Breaking up the fight, Prince Escalus lectures Montague and Capulet for the violence and hate they have brought to Verona and threatens the death penalty to anyone who breaks the peace in the future.

After the fight is over, Montague and his wife ask Benvolio about the whereabouts of their son, Romeo. Benvolio says he saw Romeo that morning, and Romeo had been acting depressed. Just then, Romeo appears. The Montagues leave quickly so Benvolio can talk with Romeo privately. Benvolio learns Romeo is sad because the woman he loves, Rosaline, does not return his affection.

Meanwhile, Capulet is meeting with Paris, a relative of the prince. Paris wants to marry Capulet's daughter, Juliet. Capulet is unsure, since she is only 13. Still, he encourages Paris to woo Juliet to discover if she might like him. He decides to throw a party, which he invites Paris to attend.

Elsewhere, Romeo and some of his friends, including Benvolio and Mercutio, a relative of the prince, are also preparing for the Capulet party. They were not invited, but are dressed in disguise because it is a masque, or costume party. At the party, Capulet welcomes everyone, including the disguised Romeo and his friends. Before long, Romeo notices a beautiful young woman in the crowd and professes to be instantly in love.

Just then, Tybalt recognizes Romeo as a Montague. Capulet notices Tybalt's anger and asks him to explain himself. Tybalt tells Capulet he has seen Romeo at the party. Not wanting a fight to occur, Capulet orders Tybalt to keep quiet about Romeo. A furious Tybalt storms out.

Romeo approaches Juliet and begins flirting with her. They kiss. Juliet's nurse interrupts them to tell Juliet her mother wishes to see her. After Juliet leaves, Romeo discovers she is a Capulet. Meanwhile, the party is ending. Juliet asks the nurse to find out Romeo's name. The nurse returns to give Juliet the bad news—Romeo is a Montague.

Act 2

After the party, Romeo sees Juliet walking out onto her balcony. Believing she is alone, Juliet professes her love for Romeo and her frustration that he is a Montague. Eventually, Romeo reveals his presence. They proclaim their love for each other and decide to get married the following day.

The next day, Romeo meets with Friar Laurence, a Catholic cleric. Romeo explains he has fallen in love with Juliet and asks the friar to unite them in marriage. Friar Laurence agrees to marry Romeo and Juliet, but he has his own motivation for doing so—he hopes marrying the young couple will end the feud between their families.

Meanwhile, Benvolio and Mercutio wonder where Romeo disappeared to after the party. Mercutio reveals Tybalt has challenged Romeo to a duel. Benvolio thinks Romeo will answer the challenge, but Mercutio is worried because Tybalt is a good fighter. Soon Romeo appears, and Romeo and Mercutio begin a vulgar banter. The nurse and a servant walk past the group, looking for Romeo. Mercutio spouts insults at the nurse until he and Benvolio leave the stage. The nurse and Romeo work out the details for the secret marriage ceremony.

In the next scene, the now-exhausted nurse arrives and tells Juliet she must go meet Friar Laurence for the wedding. In the final scene of act 2, Romeo, Juliet, and Friar Laurence meet for the marriage ceremony.

Act 3

Benvolio, Mercutio, and some other men are talking outside when Tybalt and other Capulets arrive. As Mercutio is teasing Tybalt, Romeo arrives. Tybalt wants to fight Romeo. Since he is now secretly married to Juliet, Romeo refuses, saying he loves Tybalt like a family member.

Mercutio is upset by Romeo's refusal to fight and draws his sword on Tybalt to protect Romeo's

There are many different adaptations of *Romeo and Juliet*. The 1961 musical film *West Side Story* resets the story in 1950s New York City, using modern language and character names.

honor. The two begin dueling. Romeo draws his own sword, trying to break up the fight. Tybalt uses Romeo for protection and severely wounds Mercutio. Tybalt and his friends rush away, and Mercutio dies on the street.

Tybalt returns and Romeo, angry with himself for letting Mercutio fight in his place, challenges Tybalt. The two fight, and Romeo kills Tybalt. Guards arrive to arrest the fighters, and Romeo runs away. Prince Escalus, Montague, Capulet, and their wives arrive. Benvolio recounts the fight, emphasizing Romeo's initial attempt to break it up. The Capulets want the prince to have Romeo killed, but the prince exiles him instead.

In the next scene, the nurse informs Juliet of the fight and Romeo's exile. Juliet is devastated over the death of her cousin and the banishment of her new husband. The nurse knows where Romeo is hiding and promises to bring him to Juliet that night.

Friar Laurence has been hiding Romeo and informs him the prince has banished him from Verona. Romeo despairs over the punishment. The nurse arrives to see how Romeo is doing. Friar Laurence comes up with a plan. First, Romeo and Juliet will spend the night together as planned.

Then Romeo will go live in nearby Mantua. When the time is right, Friar Laurence will make their marriage public, which will hopefully lead the Montagues and Capulets to reconcile. Romeo will then ask the prince if he can return to Verona.

In the final scene of act 3, Romeo and Juliet have spent the night together in Juliet's room. The nurse rushes in to warn them Juliet's mother is coming, and Romeo sneaks out of a distraught Juliet's room. Lady Capulet believes Juliet is upset about Tybalt's death. She tries to console her daughter by telling her the Capulets plan to hire someone to kill Romeo in Mantua. She also gives Juliet the news that she is to marry Paris in a few days. To her family's surprise, Juliet resists the marriage. Lady Capulet calls Juliet's father to talk to her. Capulet threatens to disown Juliet if she does not wed Paris. Once Juliet's parents leave, the nurse encourages Juliet to marry Paris because Romeo will soon be killed, leaving Juliet alone. Juliet pretends to agree with the nurse, but she decides to see if Friar Laurence has a better plan.

Act 4

Act 4 opens with Paris working out plans for his wedding to Juliet with Friar Laurence. Juliet arrives to talk to the friar about Romeo. She pretends to be visiting Friar Laurence to confess her sins, and Paris leaves. Once he is gone, Juliet threatens to kill herself if she is forced to marry Paris.

The friar frantically comes up with another plan. He gives Juliet a potion that will make her appear lifeless for 42 hours. Thinking she is dead, her family will put her body in their family tomb. The friar then tells Juliet he will write a letter to Romeo telling him of their plan, and Romeo will come to retrieve Juliet from the tomb when she wakes up.

Juliet returns home and apologizes to her father, promising to marry Paris. That night, she drinks the friar's potion. The next morning, her family finds her and believes she is dead.

Act 5

Friar Laurence's plan goes seriously awry when his messenger to Romeo is detained. Instead, Romeo learns of Juliet's death. Devastated, he buys poison and returns to Verona with the intent to kill himself in Juliet's tomb.

When Romeo arrives at the tomb, Paris is there paying his respects to Juliet. He thinks Romeo has ill intentions and confronts him. The two men fight, and Romeo kills Paris. Romeo goes into Juliet's tomb, where he drinks the poison and dies.

Friar Laurence arrives in the tomb too late to save Romeo. Juliet awakens and discovers Romeo dead. The friar and Juliet hear noise outside the tomb. Friar Laurence begs Juliet to leave with him. But she will not leave Romeo's side, and the friar departs alone. Hearing the watchmen draw closer, Juliet picks up Romeo's dagger, stabs herself in the chest, and dies.

Seconds later, Prince Escalus, Capulet, and Montague arrive at the tomb. Friar Laurence, who has been apprehended and returned to the tomb by the watchmen, tells the story of Romeo and Juliet's secret marriage and untimely deaths. Seeing the tragic results of the feud between their families, Capulet and Montague promise to reconcile.

Essential Critiques

Romeo and Juliet eventually marry, but their happiness is short-lived.

How to Apply Marxist Criticism to *Romeo and Juliet*

What Is Marxist Criticism?

Marxist criticism is named after Karl Marx, a German theorist who worked in the mid- to late-1800s. Marx examined issues related to class status and power. He noted how the capitalist economic system of his time made it possible for the upper class to keep the lower class at a disadvantage. He believed the lower class was being oppressed.

Marxist critics still study class and status today. They recognize, as Marx did, that there is still a great disparity among classes. In the United States, it is a common misconception that if people work hard enough, everyone should be able to provide for themselves and their families. However, people usually maintain the same class status for their entire lives. This means people born into poverty will likely remain in poverty, often despite their hard work and attempts to change their position. Marxist critics are interested in works of art that preserve or challenge stereotypes and assumptions about class. They believe a literary work will reflect the class struggles of the time it was produced. Marxist critics are also often interested in characters that overcome oppression.

Applying Marxist Criticism to *Romeo and Juliet*

In Shakespeare's *Romeo and Juliet*, two young teenagers attempt to be together despite the feud between their two families. Some of the play's characters aid the young couple in their plan to marry. Others impede their plan. The majority of these characters perform their roles in fulfillment of their social class when they help or hinder the young couple. The people around Romeo and Juliet adhere to the roles prescribed for their status in society, but in doing so they fail to prevent the tragic death of the couple and reveal the pitfalls of the status structure.

Thesis Statement

At the end of the first paragraph, the author states the thesis: "The people around Romeo and Juliet adhere to the roles prescribed for their status in society, but in doing so they fail to prevent the tragic death of the couple and reveal the pitfalls of the status structure." The essay discusses how strict social classes led to Romeo's and Juliet's deaths.

As Juliet's caregiver, the nurse's job is to care for Juliet's immediate health and well-being. Her status prevents her from seeing and acting on the broader implications of Juliet's desire for Romeo. The nurse seems to be aware that marrying Romeo could put Juliet in danger. When she is sent to arrange the marriage details, she admits to Romeo she has told Juliet, "Paris is the properer man."[1] Although the nurse prefers Paris for Juliet, she knows Juliet would rather be with Romeo and consequently aids Juliet. After all, her job as Juliet's nurse is to see to Juliet's immediate wants and needs. The nurse is not responsible for Juliet's future, only her immediate happiness.

The nurse's position does not require her to think about whether Juliet's marriage to Romeo is appropriate for the Capulet family. If she did, she would overstep the bounds of her status. So instead, the nurse remains true to her position and supports Juliet's desire to enter into a dangerous marriage to a family enemy. By simply fulfilling the role

> **Argument One**
> Next, the author presents the first argument: "As Juliet's caregiver, the nurse's job is to care for Juliet's immediate health and well-being. Her status prevents her from seeing and acting on the broader implications of Juliet's desire for Romeo." The author begins by discussing the nurse.

Juliet's nurse is one of the few characters in the play who supports Juliet in her marriage to Romeo.

assigned to her status in society without considering the bigger picture, the nurse fails to keep Juliet out of harm's way.

The Capulets also fail to protect their daughter by narrowly performing the roles expected of their status. As members of a higher social class, it is important the Capulets marry their only daughter to a man worthy of her rank. Lady Capulet shows this importance when discussing the matter with Juliet early in the play. She puts Paris's marriage proposal to Juliet quite bluntly, "Thus then, in brief: / The valiant Paris seeks you for his love."[2] It is not Lady Capulet's job to worry about whether Juliet is in love with or desires Paris; the nurse is the one concerned with Juliet's immediate happiness. Lady Capulet only needs to match her daughter with someone worthy of the family status. She is performing the role expected of a woman of nobility. However, it is this businesslike attitude toward marriage that Juliet rebels against, eventually pushing her toward her own downfall and death.

Neither is it Capulet's job to pay attention to Juliet's emotional desires. But initially, Capulet seems concerned for his daughter's happiness.

> **Argument Two**
> The author then presents the second argument: "The Capulets also fail to protect their daughter by narrowly performing the roles expected of their status." In this argument, the author focuses on Juliet's parents' social status.

When first discussing the potential marriage with Paris, Capulet wants to make sure Juliet likes Paris by throwing a party so the two can meet. However, when Juliet refuses to marry Paris, her father responds angrily, threatening to throw her out of the house. As with Lady Capulet, Capulet is performing the role expected of a man of his status. It is his responsibility to ensure his household will prosper after his death. To do so, he needs a stable son-in-law of nobility, a role Paris is ideally equipped to fill. Capulet's frustrated and rash response to Juliet pushes her further from her parents and closer to Romeo and her eventual tragic fate.

Friar Laurence performs the role expected of his status as a moral man of God whose first concern is the welfare of his community, but he sacrifices Romeo and Juliet for his cause. Although the friar agrees to marry Romeo and Juliet for their happiness, he also has his own reason for performing the union. The friar thinks marrying them could end the fighting between their families.

Argument Three

The author is now shifting to focus on the friar's role with the next argument: "Friar Laurence performs the role expected of his status as a moral man of God whose first concern is the welfare of his community, but he sacrifices Romeo and Juliet for his cause."

He explains to Romeo, "For this alliance may so happy prove / To turn your households' rancor to pure love."[3] The friar's secret motives are greater than those he has for pleasing Romeo. He wants to end the feud between the Montagues and Capulets, bringing harmony to Verona. He is performing his job as a holy man, trying to ensure peace within the community. However, in his attempt, he leads young Romeo and Juliet down a dangerous path.

Later, when Juliet wakes to find Romeo dead in the tomb, Friar Laurence is faced with a personal dilemma. He has a chance to either save Juliet's life or himself, as he hears a crowd approaching outside. But the friar's morality only goes so far, and he cowardly hides from the approaching Capulets and Montagues while Juliet takes her own life. The friar will not risk his own well-being to save Juliet. In this way, he deviates from his role as a self-sacrificing holy man. Still, it was the friar's plan, motivated by his position, which allowed Romeo and Juliet to wed in the first place. Romeo and Juliet become sacrifices to the friar's righteous fight for peace.

Although the characters around Romeo and Juliet are fulfilling the roles prescribed to their

Conclusion
The final paragraph is the conclusion. The author summarizes the arguments and partially restates the thesis. The conclusion reiterates the Marxist idea that strict class structures negatively affect society.

respective statuses, the play ends in tragedy. This demonstrates how those who blindly accept their class roles can fail to see the broader implications of their actions or lack of action. The characters are unable to keep the young couple from their eventual fate because the kind of help the couple really needs is not assigned to anyone in their community. The strict class structure limits the characters, resulting in the deaths of Romeo and Juliet and showing how such a structure can negatively affect society as a whole.

Thinking Critically about *Romeo and Juliet*

Now it is your turn to assess the critique. Consider these questions:

1. Do you agree with the author's thesis? Can you think of any evidence from the play that could disprove the author's claims?

2. What parts of the author's argument did you find most convincing? Is there any evidence you could add to this critique to strengthen the author's argument?

3. The author discusses status roles in this essay. What do you think Romeo's and Juliet's behavior might say about their roles in the upper class?

Other Approaches

A critique can be applied to a book or a play in many different ways. The previous essay is just one example of a Marxist critique of *Romeo and Juliet*. Prince Escalus is of a higher social class, and yet he behaves in a moral fashion. Another approach might examine the prince's role as an upper-class figure in the play. Yet another approach might apply a Marxist critique from a different angle, focusing on the idea that the lower classes are represented as inferior in intelligence to the upper classes.

Wealth Requires Social Obligation

Like the Montagues and Capulets, Prince Escalus has a great deal of power and money. However, unlike the wealthy families, he also has an obligation to the citizens he rules. Time and again he is seen attempting to keep the peace within his community. A thesis for this approach could be: *Romeo and Juliet* asserts that people with wealth have a social obligation to use their wealth to be productive, helpful members of their community. A supporting argument could discuss the prince's sympathy to the families upon hearing of Romeo's and Juliet's deaths.

Lower Class Lacks Intelligence

Another Marxist critique might consider class from a different angle. Although Friar Laurence and the nurse do everything they can to help Romeo and Juliet, their plans enable the eventual tragedy. Furthermore, they are often portrayed as somewhat dim-witted and strange. A thesis statement for a critique perpetuating classist ideas could be:

Friar Laurence and the nurse's willingness to help Romeo and Juliet with their dangerous plot to marry supports the stereotype that members of the lower classes are not very intelligent.

Actor Kevin Spacey portrayed a deformed Richard III in a 2011 stage version of the play.

5

An Overview of
Richard III

In *Richard III*, Shakespeare recounts the story of a real-life king of England. When Shakespeare wrote the play, the real Richard III had been dead for more than 100 years. Many details of Richard's life are portrayed inaccurately.

Act 1

Act 1 opens with Richard, the Duke of Gloucester, complaining that the English kingdom is at peace. Richard wants to be king and has already laid a plot to make his brother King Edward IV become suspicious of their brother George, Duke of Clarence. Following up on Richard's accusations, King Edward IV has sent Clarence to jail in the Tower of London.

Richard's plan is to have Clarence killed to get closer in the line of succession to the throne. Next, Richard plans to marry Lady Anne, whose husband he has killed in battle, and whose status will cement his claim to the throne. Anne does not like Richard, but he convinces her to marry him.

In a later scene, King Edward's wife, Queen Elizabeth, reveals to her supporters that she is starting to suspect something is amiss. She has been distrustful of Richard for a long time. She is worried about what will happen if the very sick King Edward dies. She is particularly concerned for the safety of her two young sons, who are in the direct line of succession to the English throne.

Attempting to avert a conflict, King Edward has charged the Duke of Buckingham and Lord Stanley, the Earl of Derby, to reconcile Richard with Elizabeth's family. Richard storms in, pretending to be furious that King Edward would think he does not like Elizabeth and her relatives. Richard blames Elizabeth for the imprisonment of Clarence in the tower, though Elizabeth denies any involvement. She does not like Richard's scheming.

The scene is further complicated by an outburst from Queen Margaret, the widow of Henry VI (the king Edward IV deposed), who sneaks onto the stage. The group is surprised to see Margaret, as she has been banished from the kingdom after the deposition. She curses everyone in the room with terrible fates. She also warns them, especially Elizabeth, that Richard is up to no good. Margaret takes Buckingham aside and warns him about Richard. Then she exits, leaving everyone in distress. Undaunted, Richard hires two assassins, who kill Clarence in prison.

Act 2

Act 2 opens with King Edward attempting to reconcile the feuding factions in his court. Richard makes a speech, professing his love to Elizabeth's family. Elizabeth asks King Edward to free Clarence and apologize to him. Richard pretends to be surprised and reveals that Clarence is dead, supposedly on the king's orders. The already ill King Edward is horrified, and his health seems to worsen.

In the next scene, the Duchess of York (the mother of King Edward, Clarence, and Richard) is watching over Clarence's young daughter and son. Elizabeth comes in, revealing King Edward has died.

Richard III is loosely based on the life of the real King Richard III, who ruled from 1483 to 1485.

Richard and Buckingham, along with others, then arrive on the scene. Richard pretends to comfort Elizabeth and his mother. Buckingham, now Richard's ally, points out that someone must go and fetch King Edward's oldest son, Prince Edward, who is next in line to be king. Richard and Buckingham decide to retrieve the prince themselves.

Meanwhile, Elizabeth and the Duchess of York discover Richard and Buckingham have had Elizabeth's supporters imprisoned. Elizabeth decides it is time to seek sanctuary in a church with her young children.

Act 3

Young Prince Edward arrives in London, wanting to know why his mother's relatives are not there to greet him. Richard claims they are bad people, but he does not tell the prince he has imprisoned them. Hastings arrives and reveals that the prince's mother and his brother have taken sanctuary and will not be coming to greet him either. Buckingham insists Elizabeth's other son, the Duke of York, be taken from sanctuary to see his brother, Prince Edward. On Richard's order, both young princes are accommodated in the tower until Prince Edward's crowning.

Richard continues to plot for the crown, intending to kill anyone who stands in his way. Once he is king, Richard promises to reward Buckingham for his service with the title Earl of Herefold. Elizabeth's allies are led to their executions, ordered by Richard.

Richard and Buckingham must make the English people accept Richard as the rightful king.

Richard asks Buckingham to deliver speeches throughout the kingdom, questioning the young princes' eligibility to rule and suggesting Queen Elizabeth had been unfaithful to the king, making the two princes illegitimate. Buckingham's speeches do not go well. People do not want Richard to be king, which makes Richard furious. Richard and Buckingham take another approach. They persuade the mayor of London to ask Richard publicly, supposedly on behalf of the people, to be king. During this staged charade, Richard acts like he does not want the honor. As part of the trick, Buckingham begs Richard to become king, and Richard finally accepts.

Act 4

Act 4 opens with Elizabeth and her supporters, including Richard's wife, Anne, trying to visit the princes in the tower. They are blocked from entering. Just then, a messenger arrives and summons Anne to her husband, announcing that Richard is being crowned king.

Although Richard is now king, he does not feel safe from being overthrown. He asks a supporter to spread rumors that Queen Anne is unwell. He orders her to be confined, planning to have her killed.

Richard now wants to marry the younger Elizabeth of York, who is the daughter of Elizabeth and the late King Edward. He also makes arrangements for King Edward's sons, the princes, to be murdered.

Even after being crowned king, Richard does not feel secure and murders everyone in his path.

But Richard's right-hand man, Buckingham, is starting to doubt him. He asks Richard to bestow the promised earldom on him, but Richard says he is not in the mood. Buckingham realizes Richard no longer considers him an ally, and he decides to flee before Richard kills him too.

Richard becomes openly ruthless in consolidating his power. He has the princes murdered and reveals that Anne, too, is dead. Now, Richard just has to marry young Elizabeth. However, some of Richard's allies, including Buckingham, have fled. Buckingham is now raising an army against Richard. Richard decides to form his own army.

In the next scene, Elizabeth and the Duchess of York mourn the princes. They are joined by former queen Margaret, who expresses joy that her curses have come true. Richard arrives, planning to ask Elizabeth for her young daughter's hand in marriage. He is met with sharp criticism of his murderous actions and is disowned by his mother. Slightly shaken, he continues to plead his case to marry young Elizabeth. Eventually, Richard seems to convince Elizabeth to talk to her daughter about the marriage. But Elizabeth is just pretending.

When they part, Richard is informed that nobles across England are raising armies against him. Buckingham's army has been conquered and Buckingham captured. Still, Richard is worried. The Earl of Richmond, the most prominent member of an enemy clan, has arrived on the coast with a large army. Richard rallies his troops and goes to battle. He does not know Elizabeth has sent an envoy to Richmond, negotiating the marriage between young Elizabeth and Richmond.

Act 5

Act 5 opens with Buckingham's execution. His death does not slow the progress of Richmond's troops, and Richard and his soldiers prepare for battle. Although Richard's numbers are larger, Richmond's troops quickly conquer Richard's.

Richmond and Richard finally meet. They battle, and Richmond kills Richard. Richmond becomes the new king and plans to marry young Elizabeth. Although the damage Richard has done will always be remembered, peace has been restored to the kingdom.

Essential Critiques

Annette Benning plays Queen Elizabeth, who uses her political skills
to undermine Richard, in the 1995 film adaptation of *Richard III*.

How to Apply Feminist Criticism to *Richard III*

What Is Feminist Criticism?

Feminist criticism analyzes the way women are portrayed in a work. Are women powerful and confident? Or are they damsels in distress waiting to be rescued by male characters? A feminist critic might consider how the portrayal of women in a work reflects or informs how a society views women.

Applying Feminist Criticism to *Richard III*

Richard III presents a world in which women first seem to be at the mercy of the men around them. Their husbands and sons die in battle or are assassinated, and they are left to pick up the pieces. However, *Richard III* also presents women as strong leaders who become notable adversaries of Richard in his plot for the crown. They become

Thesis Statement

At the end of the first paragraph, the author states her thesis: "Through their efforts to undermine Richard's plot, it is clear the women in *Richard III* are able to outsmart the men, showing their superior leadership." The essay shows how women in *Richard III* are superior leaders.

Argument One

The author begins to support her thesis with her first argument, which focuses on Queen Margaret: "Margaret, though grief stricken and perhaps a little out of her mind, emerges as the most insightful character in the play."

valuable assets in overthrowing him. Through their efforts to undermine Richard's plot, it is clear the women in *Richard III* are able to outsmart the men, showing their superior leadership.

Margaret, though grief stricken and perhaps a little out of her mind, emerges as the most insightful character in the play. Margaret uses her intuition, based on her own life experience, to predict the characters' fates. When Margaret gives her prophecies, she is providing the new leaders with a powerful warning. Using her curses, she predicts what will become of them if their quests for power go unchallenged. Margaret denounces Richard as a villain long before the other characters realize the depth of his malice. However, Margaret's warnings are ignored and she is thought to be crazy. When Buckingham brushes off her warning about Richard, Margaret points out his foolishness, "What, dost thou scorn me for my gentle counsel, / And soothe the devil that I warn thee from?"[1] But as Richard's plots come to fruition, the characters realize they should have listened to Margaret. They are surprised by the events as they unravel, events Margaret predicted from the start.

Like Margaret, Queen Elizabeth exhibits more political intelligence than many of the male characters. Early in the play, Elizabeth demonstrates an awareness of Richard's plotting and tries to alert others to the dangers of his potential reign. Near the play's final scene, Elizabeth and the Duchess of York denounce Richard as a villain. More than any character before or after her—including Richmond—Elizabeth fearlessly criticizes Richard's political strategies and demands he answer for his crimes. She taunts him, "Tell me thou villain-slave, where are my children?"[2] The duchess joins in Elizabeth's berating of Richard, and he has to strike up a band to drown out their accusations. Richard's reaction shows he acknowledges Elizabeth's and the

> **Argument Two**
> Now the author presents her second argument, shifting the focus from Queen Margaret to Queen Elizabeth: "Like Margaret, Queen Elizabeth exhibits more political intelligence than many of the male characters."

duchess's ability to threaten his power. However, he allows these criticisms to go unpunished because he ultimately believes the women are powerless.

Argument Three

The author's third argument states: "In the play's final scenes, Elizabeth beats Richard at his own game of manipulation." The author begins by showing how Elizabeth stands up to Richard.

In the play's final scenes, Elizabeth beats Richard at his own game of manipulation. When Richard proclaims he will marry Elizabeth's daughter, the young Elizabeth of York, Elizabeth resists strongly. She matches Richard line by line in her argument against this union:

KING RICHARD. *Say, I will love [Elizabeth of York] everlastingly.*

QUEEN ELIZABETH. *But how long shall that title 'ever' last?*

KING RICHARD. *Sweetly in force unto her fair life's end.*

QUEEN ELIZABETH. *But how long fairly shall her sweet life last?*[3]

Finally, Elizabeth convinces Richard she will do as he says, but instead plans to marry her daughter to the Earl of Richmond, whom she recognizes as the likely winner of the conflict. Richard does not suspect her, brushing her off as a "relenting fool, and shallow, changing woman."[4] Elizabeth outsmarts the master villain.

While the women of *Richard III* use their intuition and wits, the men use violence and manipulation to get power, which they want for their own glory, not the good of the people. The most obvious example of this is Richard. He lies, cheats, and murders his way to the throne. Richard does not care about the good of his people. He appears to enjoy the suffering he inflicts on those around him, admitting, "I am determined to prove the villain."[5] Richard's allies, who are all men, follow his example. They are equally selfish in their motives. Buckingham, for example, is only helping Richard because he hopes to be awarded an earldom.

Even Richmond, who is portrayed as the hero, fails to match the standards of leadership Elizabeth represents. Although

> **Argument Four**
> The author is supporting her thesis with her fourth argument by discussing why the men are not good leaders: "While the women of *Richard III* use their intuition and wits, the men use violence and manipulation to get power, which they want for their own glory, not the good of the people."

> **Argument Five**
> The author presents her fifth and final argument: "Even Richmond, who is portrayed as the hero, fails to match the standards of leadership Elizabeth represents." The author shows that Richmond is not the true hero of the play.

Richmond opposes Richard on the battlefield, refusing to allow him to take his kingdom, his motivations are not as selfless as Elizabeth's. By opposing Richard, Richmond becomes king, gaining almost absolute power. Elizabeth may not have anything to gain from speaking out against Richard. With her husband dead, her future is uncertain whether or not Richard remains in power. Still, she speaks out against Richard, then willingly offers her own daughter to Richmond, knowing the alliance will bring peace to the kingdom. However, there is no indication as to the kind of husband Richmond will be or whether or not he will ultimately be a better leader than Richard.

In a play focusing on power-hungry Richard, the women's use of intuition and intelligence shows them as better, more discerning leaders. Elizabeth's shrewd, political handling of Richard in the play's final scenes sets the kingdom on the path to peace. In a play with relatively few female characters, it is the women to whom Shakespeare has given the subtle power needed to defeat Richard.

Conclusion

The last paragraph of a critique should act as a conclusion. This should summarize the arguments and thesis of the essay. This essay concludes that Shakespeare gave the women of the play the power needed to overthrow Richard.

Thinking Critically about *Richard III*

Now it is your turn to assess the critique. Consider these questions:

1. Do you agree with the author's thesis? Why or why not?

2. Could you add arguments about other female characters in the play to this critique? Is Lady Anne, who gives in easily to Richard's wooing, also a better leader than the men?

3. Why do you think the other characters do not listen to Queen Margaret?

Other Approaches

There is no single right way to critique a work. Within feminist criticism, there are many different ways to consider a work. For *Richard III*, another approach could focus on the stereotype that women are more peaceful than men and the way this idea is portrayed in the play. Yet another approach could examine in greater detail the role of Queen Margaret, the only woman in the play beyond the influence of males.

Women as Peaceful

A feminist approach addressing the stereotype of women as more peaceful than men could compare the women's lack of violence to the men's extreme use of force. A thesis statement for a critique using this approach could be: In *Richard III*, women represent and encourage peace in the kingdom, reinforcing the stereotype that women are more peaceful than men. A supporting argument could demonstrate Richmond's personification of peace as female in the final lines of the play when he exclaims, "Now civil wounds are stopped; peace lives again. That she may long live here, God say 'Amen.'"[6]

Queen Margaret's Separation from the Patriarchy

Another feminist critique could include an in-depth analysis of Queen Margaret's portrayal in *Richard III*. The deaths of her son and husband have made Margaret an outcast. However, the deaths of the men in her life have also freed her from the patriarchy of the kingdom. A thesis statement for a critique that uses this approach could be: Queen Margaret's separation from the patriarchy after the death of her son and husband allows her to speak with an agency she would not otherwise have. A supporting argument could demonstrate how Margaret's freedom gave her the confidence to speak out and warn the other characters of the dangers that would soon befall them.

Shakespeare's characters are often adapted. A 2010 film version of *The Tempest* features a female Prospero.

7

An Overview of
The Tempest

Act 1

In the opening scene of *The Tempest*, a group
of nobles, including Alonso, Sebastian, Ferdinand,
Gonzalo, and Antonio, and their servants are on a
ship caught in a horrible storm.

On a nearby island Prospero, the exiled Duke of
Milan, and his daughter, Miranda, discuss the storm
they have just witnessed and which was, apparently,
orchestrated by Prospero. Prospero tells Miranda
everyone survived. With his former enemies about
to arrive on the island, he reveals to her their
history, which he has long kept a secret.

Prospero explains how his interest in studies
of the supernatural kept him from his duties as
duke. His brother, Antonio, resented having to
do all the work without the formal title. With the

aid of Alonso, the king of Naples, Antonio forced Prospero and Miranda, who was then three years old, to leave Milan. Gonzalo was the only loyal noble who helped them, giving them provisions and some of Prospero's books. They eventually arrived at their present island, where Prospero enslaved its few inhabitants, Caliban and Ariel.

After finishing his story, Prospero charms Miranda to sleep and calls for Ariel, his fairy servant who had assisted him in creating the storm. Ariel reports the noblemen and their servants have been swept overboard, but they are all alive and scattered on the island. He then reminds Prospero of his promise to free him. Prospero calls Ariel ungrateful and reminds him that he saved Ariel from a tree in which the former mistress of the island, the witch Sycorax, had imprisoned him. Threatened with being put back into the tree, Ariel promises to be obedient. Prospero says he will release Ariel in two days if he behaves himself.

Once Ariel is gone, Prospero wakes Miranda. They go to find Caliban, Sycorax's son who Prospero has enslaved. Caliban is angry; he feels he owned the island before Prospero and his daughter arrived. However, Prospero declares he has treated

Caliban fairly and generously. He claims Caliban
tried to rape Miranda, justifying his enslavement.

Meanwhile, Ariel charms Ferdinand into
following him to Miranda and Prospero. Ferdinand
is the son of the king of Naples and thinks everyone
who was on the ship with him has died. Prompted
by her father, Miranda is instantly attracted to
Ferdinand. He likes her too. Although this is part
of Prospero's plan, he does not want them to act on
their attraction to each other. He makes Ferdinand
perform hard physical labor in an effort to earn
his daughter and keep the young man occupied.
Ferdinand readily consents.

Act 2

On another part of the island, the group of
shipwrecked nobles stumbles about. King Alonso
grieves for his missing son, Ferdinand. An invisible
Ariel charms some of the nobles to sleep, but wakes
everyone up when two of them start causing trouble.
The nobles decide to search for Ferdinand.

In the next scene, Caliban imagines Prospero
has sent spirits to torment him. He sees Trinculo,
Alonso's jester shipwrecked in the storm,
approaching. Believing Trinculo to be an evil spirit,

Caliban lies flat on the ground, hoping to hide under his cloak. Trinculo comes upon Caliban's body and decides Caliban is an islander who has been killed by lightning from an approaching storm. Trinculo takes cover from the storm by crawling under Caliban's cloak. The two are found by another shipwrecked servant, Alonso's butler, Stefano, who is thoroughly intoxicated. Stefano thinks the combination of Trinculo and Caliban is a new species of humanlike animal, which he hopes to capture. Stefano believes a drink of alcohol will calm the creature down, so he gives Caliban a sip from the bottle he is carrying. Soon Stefano recognizes Trinculo. They are both happy to see each other alive.

Caliban, now intoxicated himself, thinks Stefano and Trinculo are powerful creatures and hopes they can overthrow Prospero. Stefano plays along, and Caliban begs to serve him, starting with providing the two of them with food.

Act 3

Act 3 opens with Ferdinand doing chores for Prospero. Miranda comes to visit him, and Prospero watches from a hiding place. Miranda and

Ferdinand admit their love for each other and want to get married.

Meanwhile, Stefano, Trinculo, and Caliban have been roaming about the island intoxicated. Caliban asks Stefano to kill Prospero for him. If Stefano does this, Caliban will let him rule the island and will serve him. They are overheard by the invisible Ariel who plans to warn Prospero. To keep an eye on the three men, Ariel plays music as he leaves, inducing the men to follow him.

In the next scene, the exhausted nobles give up their search for Ferdinand, assuming he has drowned. Prospero, hiding nearby, uses his magic to play music and make spirits bring the survivors a table of food. The men are astonished. Alonso, Sebastian, and Antonio approach the table and suddenly, Ariel appears. The men draw their swords, but Ariel uses magic to make their swords too heavy to lift. Ariel accuses the three men of running Prospero and Miranda out of Milan and disappears.

Act 4

In the opening scene of act 4, Prospero gives Ferdinand permission to marry Miranda. Then he has Ariel summon spirits and goddesses to entertain the couple. In the middle of the performance, Prospero remembers the plot against his life. He quickly ends the show. He sends Miranda and Ferdinand away and asks Ariel to set up a trap for the rebels, using royal clothing as bait. Prospero and Ariel become invisible and wait for the men. Soon, the trio approaches. Although Caliban warns them it is a trick, Stefano and Trinculo fall for Prospero's bait. As they are putting on the clothes, a group of spirit hounds, summoned by Ariel and Prospero, attack and chase the men away.

Act 5

In the opening scene of act 5, Ariel again reminds Prospero of the promise to free him. Ariel also informs Prospero he has imprisoned the other shipwrecked men. Prospero has Ariel fetch the men. While Ariel is gone, Prospero promises that after this last act of magic he will give up magic entirely. Ariel returns with Alonso, Gonzalo, Sebastian, Antonio, and the other nobles. They are charmed by magic and enter a magic circle Prospero has created. Prospero lectures them and praises Gonzalo for his loyalty. Prospero uncharms the men. He forgives Antonio but demands his dukedom back.

As with Shakespeare's other romance plays, *The Tempest* includes a love story, a happy ending, and surprising or fantastic elements.

Prospero then reveals both Miranda and Ferdinand, explaining the couple is now married. Alonso apologies for his favoritism to Antonio, and Prospero claims to forgive him. Prospero has Ariel find Trinculo, Caliban, and Stefano and orders them to clean the clothing they tried to steal. Then Prospero explains that in the morning everyone will return to Naples where he will again be duke. He finally frees Ariel.

As the others leave the stage, Prospero announces he no longer has his magical powers, having drowned his magical book. He asks the audience to release him from the stage with their clapping as the play ends.

Caliban, who is native to the island, views the island as his own and resents his enslavement.

How to Apply Postcolonial Criticism to *The Tempest*

What Is Postcolonial Criticism?

The term *postcolonial* refers to a community that was once colonized but later gained its independence. Critics often use postcolonial theory to look at work created by people from colonial or postcolonial regions or work about people who live in such areas. Critics may analyze how a work conveys other issues related to colonization, including oppression and identity.

Applying Postcolonial Criticism to *The Tempest*

Before *The Tempest* begins, Prospero has already landed on and colonized the island. The original inhabitants, Ariel and Caliban, are trapped on the island as slaves and subject to harsh treatment from Prospero. *The Tempest* supports the idea that colonization is a harmful practice and that freedom is essential for all people.

Although Ariel's magical powers are at least equal to Prospero's, Prospero continually reminds Ariel of his debt to him as a means of controlling him. When Ariel first asks for his freedom in Act One, Prospero reminds him of his history, "Hast thou forgot / The foul witch Sycorax . . . Hast thou forgot her?"[1] Prospero purposely insults Ariel's intelligence by implying Ariel may not remember why he is in Prospero's power. Of course Ariel could not have forgotten his past as Sycorax's prisoner. Prospero is trying to prove how much better Ariel's life is now, and Ariel's feeling of debt to Prospero likely keeps him from fighting back with his own magic.

Without Ariel's help, Prospero would not succeed in ruling the island. Ariel is an expert at performing magic for Prospero. It is Ariel who warns Prospero of Caliban's plot against his life. Although Prospero's powers seem to come from a book, Ariel's powers are innate. Ariel could overthrow Prospero, but Prospero has convinced Ariel that he has the power to imprison him again, and that Ariel owes Prospero for improving his life. Still, Ariel recognizes his own position as unfair. He repeatedly asks Prospero to release him, and is largely obedient to Prospero because Ariel believes Prospero will eventually reward him with his freedom.

Prospero's treatment of Caliban is also portrayed as harsh and unfair. Prospero runs the island and forces Caliban to do chores for him, including

> **Argument Two**
> The author now focuses on how Caliban is treated: "Prospero's treatment of Caliban is also portrayed as harsh and unfair."

making fires and finding wood. Caliban curses his enslavement, telling Prospero, "This island's mine, by Sycorax my mother, / Which thou tak'st from me."[2] Prospero declares Caliban is lying about owning the island. He also claims Caliban wanted to rape his daughter. Prospero says Caliban did not know anything until Prospero taught him things, including Prospero's language. However, Caliban never asked Prospero to teach him anything, and any knowledge Prospero may have bestowed on Caliban has not improved Caliban's life.

Caliban's violent anger and attempts at revenge illustrate the harm colonization can inflict on a culture. Despite what Prospero may believe, Caliban does not obey Prospero simply because he does not know any better. Caliban explains in his first appearance onstage, "I must obey.

Argument Three

Now, the author builds on argument two with argument three: "Caliban's violent anger and attempts at revenge illustrate the harm colonization can inflict on a culture." The author examines Caliban's anger at his enslavement.

[Prospero's] art is of such power / It would control my dam's god Setebos, / And make a vassal of him."[3] Caliban is smart, and he realizes Prospero's magic can overpower him. Still, he attempts to reason with Prospero, citing his own birthright to the island. However, Caliban is ignored. Frustrated by his circumstances as a slave to Prospero, Caliban resorts to violence to try to change his situation. Caliban's long enslavement has depleted his ability to make his own choices. Additionally, years of Prospero's belittlements and orders have taken a toll

on his self-confidence. Rather than trying to devise a plan on his own, Caliban teams up with Stefano and Trinculo. Caliban's choice of these foolish drunkards as his allies shows just how desperate he has become. His plot to kill Prospero illustrates the negative consequences that can occur when humans try to control other humans.

Ariel, *left*, remains loyal to Prospero, *right*, for the entire play. He is rewarded with his freedom.

<u>Prospero's epilogue reinforces the importance of freedom for all people.</u> Throughout the play, Caliban and Ariel use different approaches to gain their freedom. At the play's very end, Prospero reveals himself as a servant of the stage. He asks the audience, "But release me from my bands / With the help of your good hands."[4] He wants the audience to applaud, signifying the ending of the play and Prospero's freedom from the stage. Even Prospero, who may have appeared free to the audience, was not. He too recognizes the joy of freedom.

By demonstrating freedom as the goal for many of the characters, *The Tempest* shows how essential freedom is to all people. Prospero's colonization and treatment of Ariel and Caliban is portrayed as a source of psychological stress. And although Ariel and Prospero are freed at the end of the play, Caliban remains imprisoned, perhaps as a reminder of slavery's irreversible damage.

Thinking Critically about *The Tempest*

Now it is your turn to assess the critique.
Consider these questions:

1. Do you agree that *The Tempest* reveals the
    negatives of colonization? Can you think of any
    evidence from the play that could disprove the
    author's claims?

2. What parts of the author's argument did you
    find most convincing? Is there any evidence
    you could add to this critique to strengthen the
    author's argument?

3. In the conclusion, the author suggests Caliban
    remains imprisoned as a reminder of the
    hopeless life of a slave. Do you agree? What
    else might Caliban's fate represent?

Other Approaches

The previous essay is just one example of a postcolonial critique of *The Tempest*. Another approach might include a closer examination of the two characters in the play with the least freedom, Ariel and Caliban. Yet another approach might analyze how Ariel embodies the European stereotype asserting that native people are magical.

Good Slave Verses Bad Slave

In comparing Ariel and Caliban, it may seem Ariel is superior. Ariel is eventually granted his freedom, while Caliban will likely remain a slave. However, Ariel's approach to gaining his freedom reinforces the idea of good slaves being treated well. A thesis statement for a critique using this approach could be: Ariel's good behavior, in opposition to Caliban's plot to kill Prospero, supports the idea that those who collaborate with their oppressors will be rewarded. A supporting argument could demonstrate how Ariel, who is freed, never actually defies Prospero. Ariel even warns Prospero of the plot against his life.

Native People as Magical

Early explorers often stereotyped native people as magical. In *The Tempest*, Prospero has to learn magic from a book, but Ariel is a spirit and has innate magical powers. Additionally, the island is home to many other magical spirits. A thesis statement for a critique using this approach could be: *The Tempest* reinforces the common colonial idea that native people are magical, which serves as a way to classify them as strange and different from the early European explorers.

As You Like It, a story of romance and disguise, has resonated with viewers around the world for hundreds of years.

An Overview of
As You Like It

Act 1

When Shakespeare's comedy *As You Like It* begins, Sir Rowland de Bois has recently died. He had three sons: Oliver, Jaques, and Orlando. After Rowland's death, Oliver became the head of the family. Act 1 opens with Orlando complaining to Adam, a servant, about how Oliver treats him. Oliver pays for Jaques to go to school and be brought up as a gentleman, but he has not given Orlando the same opportunities.

As Orlando and Adam are talking, Oliver arrives. Orlando accuses Oliver of not recognizing him as a brother. Angered by this, Oliver physically attacks Orlando, and Orlando fights back. Orlando gains the upper hand in the fight and before releasing Oliver, he makes Oliver promise to give him some of the money their father left them. Orlando wants to make himself into a gentleman. Oliver promises to assist him, but after Orlando and Adam leave, he reveals he has no intention of giving Orlando anything.

A bit later, Oliver speaks to Charles, a wrestler for the new duke, Frederick. Charles tells Oliver how Frederick deposed his older brother, Duke Senior, and banished him and ~~his~~ supporters to the forest of Ardennes. The only one who was not exiled was Rosalind, Senior's daughter, due to her close relationship with her cousin Celia, Frederick's only child and heir. Charles explains he is supposed to wrestle in a match tomorrow and has heard a rumor that Orlando plans to disguise himself and enter the match as his opponent. Worried he will hurt Orlando, Charles hopes Oliver will step in to protect his brother. Oliver tells Charles he does not mind if Orlando is hurt because he is a horrible person.

In the next scene, Celia and Rosalind discuss Duke Senior's banishment and watch the wrestling match between Charles and Orlando. Everyone thinks Orlando will be gravely injured fighting Charles. To their astonishment, Orlando wins easily. Frederick is upset to hear Orlando is the son of Rowland, who was his enemy. However, Rosalind is delighted because her father liked Rowland. Rosalind starts showing signs of affection for Orlando, who seems to view her with equal interest. However, because of his link to Senior and the deposed camp, Orlando must leave the court quickly.

Later, Celia attempts to cheer up a sad Rosalind. Suddenly, Frederick appears and unexpectedly banishes Rosalind from the court. Both Rosalind and Celia speak out against this unfair treatment, but Frederick is unmoved. The two women make a plan to disguise themselves and go to the forest of Ardennes to find Rosalind's father. Rosalind will dress as a man and call herself Ganymede. Celia will dress as a peasant woman named Aliena. They decide to take Frederick's court fool Touchstone with them for entertainment and protection.

Act 2

Act 2 opens with Senior and his lords considering their situation in the forest of Ardennes. Jaques, one of the lords who serves Senior, has been very depressed. Senior wants to check on him.

Meanwhile, Adam and Orlando meet in the forest and begin looking for Senior's camp. Their journey is long and arduous, and Orlando eventually has to carry the old servant on his back.

In a different part of the forest, Celia, Rosalind, and Touchstone are walking. The exhausted travelers pause for a rest when Corin and Silvius, two local shepherds, come by. Silvius is complaining to Corin about his unrequited love for the shepherdess Phoebe. He runs off when Corin does not seem to understand his feelings.

Rosalind sympathizes with Silvius, as she feels the same way about Orlando. The travelers learn Corin's employer is looking to sell his land and sheep. Rosalind decides to buy the property, and the travelers settle in a small cottage.

In Senior's camp, Jaques comes to see the former duke. Jaques is happy because he met a fool, likely Touchstone, who made him laugh. Jaques decides that he, too, wants to be a fool. Without warning, Orlando appears. Drawing his sword, he demands food for himself and Adam. Orlando is surprised when Senior offers his food freely. The former duke discovers Orlando is Rowland's son and reveals his own identity to Orlando.

Act 3

Act 3 opens with Oliver realizing Orlando is missing. He tells Frederick, who orders Oliver to find his missing brother, threatening to take all of Oliver's property if he fails.

Back in the forest, Orlando is expressing his love for Rosalind by hanging love poems from the branches of trees. When Rosalind finds them, she thinks they are awful, though she is pleased by the affection they convey. Celia arrives, and they discuss the poems. As they talk, Orlando and Jaques appear. Celia and Rosalind hide to eavesdrop on what turns out to be a witty exchange of insults, followed by Jaques's departure. Seizing the opportunity to talk to Orlando, Rosalind—still dressed as Ganymede—offers to cure Orlando of his love affliction. To do so, she tells Orlando he must come and woo Ganymede every day.

In another part of the forest, Touchstone makes arrangements to marry Audrey, a poor shepherdess. Jaques is puzzled at Touchstone's choice of a wife who is below his class status.

In the next scene, Rosalind and Celia are waiting for Orlando, who is supposed to come for one of his curing sessions. Rosalind worries

Orlando's tardiness means he has been cured already. Corin appears and takes the women to observe an interaction between Phoebe and Silvius. Phoebe staunchly rejects Silvius's advances. Rosalind—dressed as Ganymede—appears and lectures Phoebe for not returning Silvius's love. Rosalind, Celia, and Corin leave, and Phoebe tells Silvius that, though she does not love him, she will allow him to court her. Phoebe also thinks Ganymede is attractive, and she is dismayed by his harsh words toward her. She decides to write a love letter to Ganymede and have Silvius deliver it.

Act 4

In act 4, Orlando finally arrives for his curing session with Ganymede, who pretends to be Rosalind while instructing him in the art of wooing. They practice being married, and Ganymede lectures Orlando on the ways a woman's behavior changes after marriage. It is not a flattering picture. Orlando disagrees, maintaining his love for Rosalind. He says he must go eat with Senior but promises to return. After Orlando leaves, Celia accuses Rosalind of misrepresenting women. Rosalind disregards Celia's objections and talks about her love for Orlando.

While Rosalind and Celia wait for Orlando's return, Silvius brings Rosalind the letter from Phoebe. Rosalind is shocked by how mean-spirited the letter is. As Ganymede, Rosalind tells Silvius to go back to Phoebe with news that Ganymede will not love Phoebe unless Phoebe loves Silvius.

As Silvius leaves, Oliver arrives and explains Orlando's absence. Oliver tells a story of how Orlando was injured saving Oliver from a lion. Orlando asked Oliver to bring his bloody handkerchief to the man who pretends to be Rosalind. At this news, Rosalind faints. Once she is revived, Celia takes her back to the cottage to rest.

Act 5

The final act opens with William, another man who is in love with Audrey, coming to claim her from Touchstone. Touchstone threatens to kill William if he tries to take her. William runs away, and Corin appears to bring Touchstone to see Celia and Rosalind.

Elsewhere, Oliver tells Orlando he loves Celia, who he thinks is a shepherdess named Aliena. Just then, Rosalind arrives dressed as Ganymede, and Oliver goes off to plan his marriage to Celia. With his brother getting married, Orlando despairs he cannot marry Rosalind. Ganymede promises that when Oliver marries Celia, Orlando will also marry Rosalind.

Phoebe and Silvius appear. Ganymede again tries to persuade Phoebe to love Silvius, but Phoebe insists she loves Ganymede. Ganymede tells everyone to meet tomorrow. She tells Orlando he will marry Rosalind. She tells Phoebe she will marry the person she loves if Ganymede would ever marry a woman. Rosalind also promises marriage to Silvius. They all agree to attend. Elsewhere, Audrey and Touchstone also plan to marry the following day.

The next day, Senior, his lords, Orlando, Oliver, and Celia—still disguised as Aliena—wait for Ganymede to arrive. Ganymede appears with Silvius and Phoebe. Ganymede makes sure the duke approves of Rosalind marrying Orlando and makes Phoebe promise to marry Silvius if Ganymede cannot marry her. Ganymede and Aliena exit the stage.

Rosalind and Celia, with Hymen, the god of marriage, return and reveal their previous disguises. Hymen performs marriage ceremonies for Celia and Oliver, Orlando and Rosalind, and Phoebe and Silvius.

After the ceremony, Jaques de Bois, Rowland's second son, arrives. He reveals that Frederick has decided to live a holy life. Because Frederick is no longer duke, Senior and everyone in his camp will be able to return to court. The other Jaques, Senior's lord, decides to follow Frederick into the monastery rather than return to court. Everyone leaves, and Rosalind delivers an epilogue.

Rosalind eventually reveals her disguise and marries Orlando.

Rosalind spends almost the entire play disguised as a man—a disguise none of the other characters see through.

How to Apply Gender Criticism to *As You Like It*

What Is Gender Criticism?

Gender criticism considers the way gender is understood in a society. Gender critics often ask how much the biological differences between sexes influences gender identity and behavior as it is defined by a society. A gender critic might try to distinguish behavior rooted in biology from behavior taught by society. A critic might also consider whether women or men have been conditioned by society to behave a certain way.

Applying Gender Criticism to *As You Like It*

In *As You Like It*, Rosalind disguises herself as Ganymede, a man, for the majority of the play. She also spends much of the play teaching Orlando the proper way to court a woman, and in the process

Thesis Statement

At the end of the first paragraph, the author states her thesis: "With its cross-dressing tricks and discussion of how men and women should behave in love, *As You Like It* promotes the idea that gender is a social performance and illustrates the inadequacy of strict gender roles." The essay focuses on the fluidity of gender roles.

Argument One

The first argument focuses on how well Rosalind performs gender: "Rosalind's male disguise easily fools everyone about her true sex, proving gender is something that can be invented and manipulated."

fashions him into an appropriate suitor for her. With its cross-dressing tricks and discussion of how men and women should behave in love, *As You Like It* promotes the idea that gender is a social performance and illustrates the inadequacy of strict gender roles.

Rosalind's male disguise easily fools everyone about her true sex, proving gender is something that can be invented and manipulated. When Orlando first meets Rosalind in the forest, she is disguised as Ganymede and he does not question her manhood. What he does question is her class, saying her "accent is something finer than you could purchase in so removed a dwelling."[1] Senior, Rosalind's own father, merely notes a faint resemblance upon seeing her as Ganymede, saying "I do remember in this shepherd boy / Some lively touches of my daughter's favour."[2] Orlando adds to the duke's response, saying "Methought he was a brother to your daughter."[3] Though the resemblance is noted, no one questions Ganymede's male identity because Rosalind performs the male gender role so convincingly.

Because gender is a performance, Rosalind, a woman with no experience in being male, can nonetheless teach Orlando how to perform his own male gender role. As a man pursuing a woman of Rosalind's status, Orlando must woo her. However, likely due to the fact he has not been brought up as a gentleman, Orlando is terrible at romance and ill equipped to court Rosalind. He knows he should express his feelings poetically, but his love poems are awful.

Because a person's gender performance does not consistently match a person's biological sex in the play, even Rosalind finds it difficult to distinguish between genders. When Rosalind reads the

Argument Two
The author's second argument states: "Because gender is a performance, Rosalind, a woman with no experience in being male, can nonetheless teach Orlando how to perform his own male gender role." The author begins by discussing how Orlando fails to perform his gender role.

Argument Three
The author's third argument speaks to the fluidity of gender: "Because a person's gender performance does not consistently match a person's biological sex in the play, even Rosalind finds it difficult to distinguish between genders."

harsh letter from Phoebe, she initially does not believe Phoebe wrote it. To Rosalind, the letter does not sound like something a woman would write. Rosalind exclaims, "Women's gentle brain / Could not drop forth such giant-rude invention."[4] Rosalind is surprised when Phoebe's letter strays from the tone she expects, proving gender can be manipulated without a physical disguise. Even Rosalind does not seem to understand how flexible gender roles are.

As You Like It shows how easily gender roles can be performed and demonstrates how difficult it is to define a gender. The shifting of gender roles throughout the play and the emphasis placed on how men and women should behave in love supports the idea of gender being social performance. It also illustrates the inadequacy of strict gender roles, calling for a more flexible definition of what it means to be a man and what it means to be a woman.

> **Conclusion**
> The final paragraph is the conclusion. The author partially restates the thesis, now backed up by the supporting arguments.

Thinking Critically about *As You Like It*

Now it is your turn to assess the critique. Consider the following questions:

1. Do you agree with the author's thesis? Can you think of any evidence from the play that could disprove the author's claims?

2. The author asserts that Rosalind performs the male gender role so well no one can tell she is female. How do other characters perform their gender without disguise? How do they characterize masculinity and femininity?

3. In the conclusion, the author suggests the need for more flexible gender roles. Do you agree?

Other Approaches

The previous essay is just one example of a gender critique of *As You Like It*. Another approach could include a deeper analysis of the significance of cross-dressing in *As You Like It*. Yet another approach could focus on Orlando's lack of masculinity due to his lack of education, illustrating gender roles can be learned.

Cross-Dressing for Power

As a woman, Rosalind's traditional gender role would dictate that she wait for Orlando to court her. Instead, Rosalind seeks him out. By taking the initiative, Rosalind assumes a traditionally masculine role. However, while doing this, Rosalind is dressed as a man. A thesis statement for a critique that uses this approach could be: By disguising herself as a man, Rosalind gains an agency she would not have had as a woman.

Learned Masculinity

In the beginning of the play, Orlando laments being denied the education of a gentleman. Later, it becomes clear Orlando cannot adequately perform the duties of his gender, including wooing Rosalind, because he never learned how to be a suitable man. A thesis statement for a critique using this approach could be: Orlando's inability to perform the duties of his gender along with his lack of education in that area promotes the idea that gender is a learned behavior. A supporting argument could analyze Rosalind's scathing reaction to Orlando's poorly written love poems.

You Critique It

Now that you have learned about different critical theories and how to apply them to literature, are you ready to perform your own critique? You have read that this type of evaluation can help you look at literature in a new way and make you pay attention to certain issues you may not have otherwise recognized. So, why not use one of the critical theories profiled in this book to consider a fresh take on your favorite book?

First, choose a theory and the book you want to analyze. Remember that the theory is a springboard for asking questions about the work.

Next, write a specific question that relates to the theory you have selected. Then you can form your thesis, which should provide the answer to that question. Your thesis is the most important part of your critique and offers an argument about the work based on the tenets, or beliefs, of the theory you are applying. Recall that the thesis statement typically appears at the very end of the introductory paragraph of your essay. It is usually only one sentence long.

After you have written your thesis, find evidence to back it up. Good places to start are in the work itself or in journals or articles that discuss what other people have said about it. Since you are critiquing a book, you may also want to read about the author's life so you can get a sense of what factors may have affected the creative process. This can be especially useful if working within historical, biographical, or psychological criticism.

Depending on which theory you are applying, you can often find evidence in the book's language, plot, or character development. You should also explore parts of the book that seem to disprove your thesis and create an argument against them. As you do this, you might want to address what other critics have written about the book. Their quotes may help support your claim.

Before you start analyzing a work, think about the different arguments made in this book. Reflect on how evidence supporting the thesis was presented. Did you find that some of the techniques used to back up the arguments were more convincing than others? Try these methods as you prove your thesis in your own critique.

When you are finished writing your critique, read it over carefully. Is your thesis statement understandable? Do the supporting arguments flow logically, with the topic of each paragraph clearly stated? Can you add any information that would present your readers with a stronger argument in favor of your thesis? Were you able to use quotes from the book, as well as from other critics, to enhance your ideas?

Did you see the work in a new light?

Timeline

1564 — William Shakespeare
is likely born on April 23;
he is baptized on April 26.

1582 — Shakespeare marries Anne Hathaway.

1583 — Shakespeare's first child,
Susanna, is born in May.

1592 — Robert Greene writes an article
that includes a negative mention
of Shakespeare as a playwright.

1594 — Shakespeare is listed as a member in the
Lord Chamberlain's Men theater group.

1596 — Shakespeare's son, Hamnet, dies.

1599 — The Globe Theater, in which
Shakespeare is a major investor, opens.

1609 — Shakespeare's sonnets
are published.

1585 Hathaway gives birth to twins, Hamnet and Judith.

Mid-1580s Shakespeare likely leaves Stratford-upon-Avon for London.

1590 Shakespeare likely begins writing plays about this time.

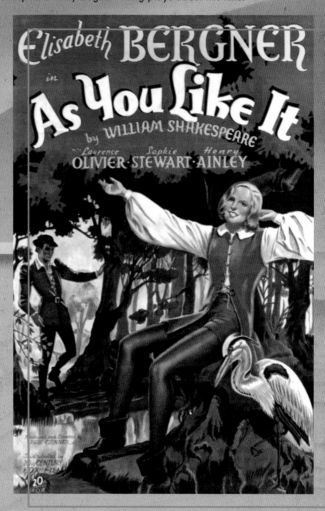

1612 Shakespeare likely retires.

1616 In March, Shakespeare makes some changes to his will; he dies on April 23.

Glossary

adversaries
Rivals.

agency
Personal power.

apprehended
Took into custody.

capitalism
An economic system that supports private companies and competition for material goods.

colonized
Took possession of a land and made it into a colony.

deposed
Removed from a throne or other high position.

exile
To banish from one's own country or home.

feud
A long-lasting fight.

gender role
A stereotype of how a person of a certain sex should act.

innate
From within.

malice
Cruelty.

patriarchy

A society in which men dominate.

reconcile

To end a fight or disagreement.

unrequited

Unreturned.

woo

To flirt or seek love.

Bibliography of Works and Criticism

Important Works

The Comedy of Errors, 1589–1594

The Two Gentlemen of Verona, 1589–1594

Richard III, 1592–1593

The Taming of the Shrew, 1593–1594

The Sonnets, 1593–1609

Romeo and Juliet, 1594–1596

Love's Labour's Lost, 1594–1595

A Midsummer Night's Dream, 1595–1596

The Merchant of Venice, 1596–1597

Much Ado About Nothing, 1598–1599

As You Like It, 1599

Julius Caesar, 1599

Hamlet, 1600–1601

Troilus and Cressida, 1600–1603

Twelfth Night, 1601–1602

Othello, 1602–1604

Measure for Measure, 1603–1604

King Lear, 1605

Macbeth, 1606

The Winter's Tale, 1609–1611

The Tempest, 1610–1611

Essential Critiques

Critical Discussions

Martin, Jennifer L. "Tights vs. Tattoos: Filmic
Interpretations of *Romeo and Juliet*." *The English
Journal*. National Council of Teachers of English,
2002: 41–46. Print.

Slights, Jessica. "Rape and Romanticization of
Shakespeare's Miranda." *Studies in English
Literature, 1500–1900*. Rice University, 2001:
357–379. Print.

Strout, Nathaniel. "*As You Like It, Rosalynde*, and
Mutuality." *Studies in English Literature, 1500–
1900*. Rice University, 2001: 277–295. Print.

Resources

Selected Bibliography

Greenblatt, Stephen. *Will in the World: How Shakespeare Became Shakespeare*. London: W.W. Norton, 2004. Print.

Shakespeare, William. "As You Like It." *The Norton Shakespeare*. London: W.W. Norton, 1997. Print.

Shakespeare, William. "The Tempest." *The Norton Shakespeare*. London: W.W. Norton, 1997. Print.

Shakespeare, William. "The Tragedy of Richard III." *The Norton Shakespeare*. London: W.W. Norton, 1997. Print.

Further Readings

Barry, Peter. *Beginning Theory: An Introduction to Literary and Cultural Theory*. Manchester: Manchester UP, 2002. Print.

Johnson, Vernon Elso, Ed. *Coming of Age in William Shakespeare's Romeo and Juliet*. Detroit: Greenhaven, 2009. Print.

Royle, Nicholas. *How to Read Shakespeare*. New York: W.W. Norton, 2005. Print.

Essential Critiques

Web Links

To learn more about critiquing the works of William Shakespeare, visit ABDO Publishing Company online at **www.abdopublishing.com**. Web sites about the works of William Shakespeare are featured on our Book Links page. These links are routinely monitored and updated to provide the most current information available.

For More Information

Folger Shakespeare Library

201 East Capitol Street, SE; Washington, DC 20003

202-544-4600

www.folger.edu

This Shakespeare research center has the largest collection of Shakespeare materials in the world.

The Royal Shakespeare Company

Waterside, Stratford-upon-Avon, Warwickshire, CV37 6BB

0844-800-1110

www.rsc.org.uk

The Royal Shakespeare Company is one of the best-known Shakespearean theater companies in the world.

Source Notes

Chapter 1. Introduction to Critiques
None.

Chapter 2. A Closer Look at William Shakespeare
None.

Chapter 3. An Overview of *Romeo and Juliet*
None.

Chapter 4. How to Apply Marxist Criticism to *Romeo and Juliet*

1. Stephen Greenblatt. Ed. *The Norton Shakespeare*.

London: W.W. Norton, 1997. 901. Line 186.

2. Ibid. 882. Lines 75–76.

3. Ibid. 896. Lines 91–92.

Chapter 5. An Overview of *Richard III*

None.

Chapter 6. How to Apply Feminist Criticism to
Richard III

   1. Stephen Greenblatt. Ed. *The Norton Shakespeare*.
London: W.W. Norton, 1997. 531. Lines 295–296.

   2. Ibid. 576. Lines 140–144.

   3. *William Shakespeare: The Complete Works*. New
York: Barnes & Noble, 1994. 130–131. Line 349.

   4. Stephen Greenblatt. Ed. *The Norton Shakespeare*.
London: W.W. Norton, 1997. 582. Line 362.

   5. Ibid. 516. Line 30.

   6. Ibid. 596. Lines 40–41.

Chapter 7. An Overview of *The Tempest*
None.

Chapter 8. How to Apply Postcolonial Criticism to *The Tempest*

1. Stephen Greenblatt. Ed. *The Norton Shakespeare*. London: W.W. Norton, 1997. 3063. Lines 259–260.

2. Ibid. 3065. Lines 334–335.

3. Ibid. 3066. Lines 375–377.

4. Ibid. 3106. Lines 9–10.

Chapter 9. An Overview of *As You Like It*

None.

Chapter 10. How to Apply Gender Criticism to *As You Like It*

1. Stephen Greenblatt. Ed. *The Norton Shakespeare*. London: W.W. Norton, 1997. 1631. Lines 310–311.

2. Ibid. 1652. Lines 26–27.

3. Ibid. 1652. Lines 28–29.

4. Ibid. 1644. Lines 33–34.

Index

About the Author

Mari Kesselring is the author and editor of many books for young people. A major Shakespeare fan, Kesselring has seen the Royal Shakespeare Company in Stratford-upon-Avon perform several plays, including *Richard III*. She also presented a critical essay about women in Shakespeare plays at a national academic conference.

Photo Credits

Georgios Kollidas/Shutterstock Images, cover, 3, 12, 98; Lance Bellers/iStockphoto, 17, 98; 20th Century Fox/Everett Collection, 18, 28; United Artists/Photofest, 23, 50; Everett Collection, 32, 47, 78, 99; Alastair Muir/Rex Features/AP Images, 40; Georgios Kollidas/iStockphoto, 44; Sue Gordon/Touchstone Pictures/Everett Collection, 60; Donald Cooper/Rex Features/AP Images, 67; Touchstone Pictures/Photofest, 68, 73; PictureHouse/Everett Collection, 87; Mary Evans/Ronald Grant/Everett Collection, 88